Searchlight
BOOKS™

How
Do Simple
Machines Work?

Put
Screws
to the Test

by Sally M. Walker and Roseann Feldmann

Lerner Publications Company
Minneapolis

For Beth Hirsch, friend forever, even
when I can't remember! —RF

Lerner Publications Company
A division of Lerner Publishing Group, Inc.
241 First Avenue North
Minneapolis, MN 55401 U.S.A.

Website address: www.lernerbooks.com

Library of Congress Cataloging-in-Publication Data

Walker, Sally M.
        Put screws to the test / by Sally M. Walker and Roseann Feldmann.
            p.   cm. — (Searchlight books™—How do simple machines work?)
        Includes index.
        ISBN 978–0–7613–5323–2 (lib. bdg. : alk. paper)
        1. Screws—Juvenile literature. I. Feldmann, Roseann. II. Title.
    TJ1338.W35 2012
    621.8'82—dc22   2010035552

Manufactured in the United States of America
1 – DP – 7/15/11

Contents

Chapter 1

WORK

You work every day.
At home, you work in
the kitchen. At school,
you sharpen pencils.
It may surprise you to
learn that you also work
during recess and at lunch.
Playing and eating are
work too!

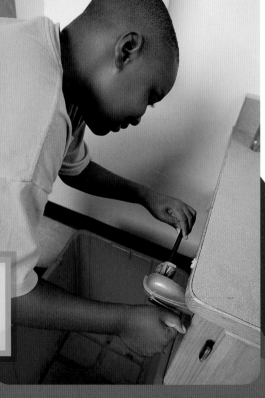

You do work when
you sharpen a pencil.
Are you working when
you play or eat?

Work = Using Force to Move an Object

When scientists use the word *work*, they don't mean the opposite of play. Work is using a force to move an object from one place to another. Force is a push or a pull. You use force to do chores, to play, and to eat.

These children are using force to climb a rope ladder.

Sometimes you push or pull an object to move it to a new place. Then you have done work. The distance that the object moves may be long or short. But the object must move. Opening a jar of peanut butter is work. Your force moves the lid.

This girl has used force to open the lid of a jar. She has done work.

Here the girl is using a lot of force to try to turn a lid. But the lid is not moving. Is the girl doing work?

Some lids are too hard to open. You have done no work if you cannot turn the lid. It's not work even if you try until your wrist feels like rubber. No matter how hard you try, you have done no work. The lid has not moved.

Chapter 2
MACHINES

Most people want to make doing work easy. Machines are tools that make work easier. Some of them make work go faster too.

An electric drill has many moving parts. What do we call a machine that has many moving parts?

Complicated Machines

Some machines have many moving parts. We call them complicated machines. It may be hard to understand how complicated machines work. Electric drills and clothes washers are complicated machines.

A clothes washer is a complicated machine.

Simple Machines

Some machines are easy to understand. They are called simple machines. Simple machines have few moving parts.

Simple machines are found in every home, school, and playground. They are so simple that most people don't realize they are machines.

This girl is turning a wheel. A wheel is a simple machine.

Chapter 3

WHAT IS A SCREW?

A screw is a simple machine. A screw looks like a nail with ridges. The ridges on a screw are called a thread.

A screw is a simple machine that looks like a nail. What is the difference between a nail and a screw?

A hammer pushes a nail into wood. Your fingers push a pin into fabric. But you don't push a screw. Instead, a screw is turned. The thread on a screw pulls the screw into the material. The material can be wood or metal. It can be Styrofoam or plastic. It can even be concrete or dirt!

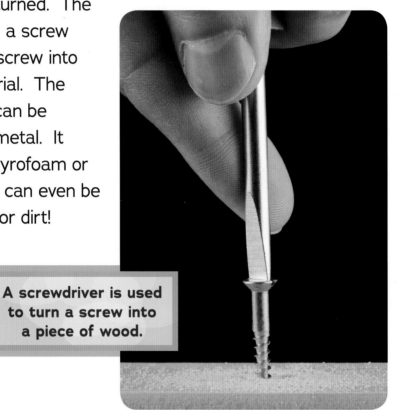

A screwdriver is used to turn a screw into a piece of wood.

A screw seems to have many threads. But it really has just one thread. You can prove this.

YOU WILL NEED A SHEET OF PAPER, A RULER, A PENCIL, A CRAYON OR A MARKER, TAPE, AND A SCISSORS.

What You Do

Make a dot at one corner of the paper. Measure 3 inches (8 centimeters) from the dot along one edge of the paper. Make an *X*. Next, measure 3 inches from the dot along the other edge of the paper. Make another *X*.

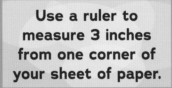

Use a ruler to measure 3 inches from one corner of your sheet of paper.

Your line should look like this when you connect the two marks.

Connect the two marks by
using a colorful crayon or marker
and the edge of the ruler. Your line will be slanted.

Use the scissors to cut just outside the line. You will have a triangle with one slanted edge that is colored.

Be sure to cut outside the line you have made.

Ask a friend to
help you wrap
the triangle
around the pencil.

Tape one plain edge of the triangle to the pencil.
Make sure you can see the colored line. Next, wrap the
triangle tightly around the pencil. Tape the end so the
paper will not unroll.

Look at your homemade screw. The colored slanted edge is the thread on your screw. The one colorful line looks like three lines wrapped around the pencil. You know there is only one thread. But it looks like more than one thread.

Your screw looks like it has several threads. But you know it has just one thread.

Chapter 4

HOW SCREWS HELP US

The neck of a jar has a thread. You can trace the thread from top to bottom. You do not have to lift your finger. So you know that the neck has just one thread.

How many threads does the neck of this jar have?

The neck of a jar is a screw. The jar's lid turns easily on the screw. The lid fits tightly on the neck of the jar. But screwing on a lid takes longer than pushing on a lid. Why does it take longer to screw on a lid?

The neck of this bottle is a screw. You cannot push the lid onto the bottle. You must turn the lid on the screw.

The thread is the reason it takes longer to screw on a lid. Why would you be willing to work longer? Sometimes working longer means the job will be done better.

A jar's thread keeps the lid from coming off.

You can prove this for yourself. Give this fun experiment a try. You'll need a Styrofoam plate, a scissors, a nail, and a screw.

THESE ITEMS WILL HELP YOU SEE HOW WORKING LONGER SOMETIMES MEANS YOU'LL DO A BETTER JOB.

What You Do

Cut the plate in half. Stack one piece on top of the other. Push the nail through both pieces. Try to pull the two pieces of Styrofoam apart. It is probably easy.

It is easy to push a nail through two pieces of Styrofoam. But the nail does not hold the two pieces together well.

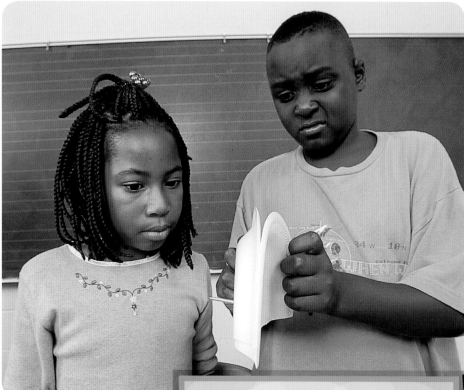

It takes longer to turn a screw into the Styrofoam than it takes to push a nail in. But the screw holds the pieces together better.

Stack the two pieces again. This time, turn the screw through both pieces. Try to pull the two pieces apart. It's hard to do. The thread on the screw keeps the screw tightly in place. The pieces of Styrofoam do not pull apart.

Jugs with Threads

The neck of some plastic jugs has a thread. If the jug is dropped, the thread holds the lid tightly in place. So the liquid stays in the jug.

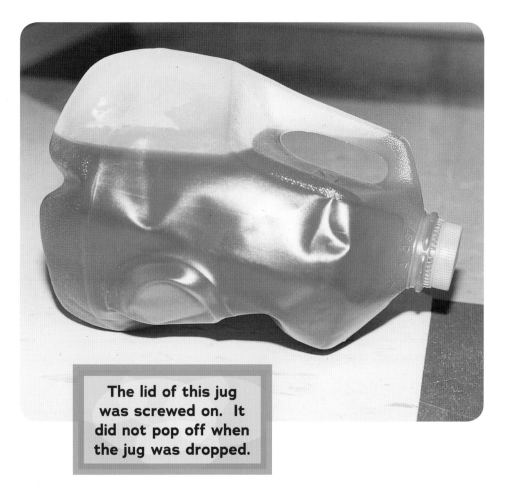

The lid of this jug was screwed on. It did not pop off when the jug was dropped.

This jug has a lid that was pushed on. The lid popped off when the jug was dropped.

Jugs without Threads

The neck of other jugs has no thread. Their lid is pushed on. The lid can pop off if the jug is dropped. Which kind of jug would you rather have land on your kitchen floor?

Screws and Door Hinges

Open a door. Look at the hinges that hold the door in its frame. Do you see nails, or do you see screws? A nail's head is smooth. A screw's head has cuts in it. You will see that screws are used on the door's hinges.

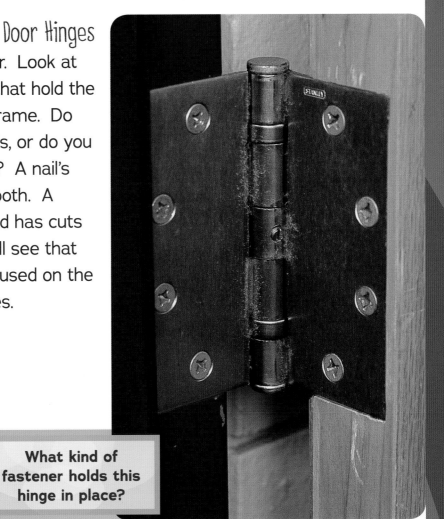

What kind of fastener holds this hinge in place?

Screws keep a door's hinges tightly in place. A door is opened and closed a lot. It would be terrible if hinges pulled out easily. A falling door would hurt people!

A door is opened and closed often. Screws keep it from falling out of its frame.

Chapter 5

KINDS OF SCREWS

Look at several different screws. How are they the same? How are they different? Count the number of thread lines on each screw. Some screws have more thread lines than others. How can you get more thread lines on a screw? You can get more thread lines by changing how steeply the thread slants.

What is the difference between these two screws?

You will need to cut a new triangle to make another homemade screw.

Let's make a new triangle. Make a dot on a different corner of the paper you have already used. Measure 3 inches (8 cm) from the dot along one edge. Make an *X*. Then measure 6 inches (15 cm) along the other edge. Make an *X*. Connect the marks by drawing a straight line. Cut out the triangle the same way you did before.

Next, tape the 3-inch (8 cm) side of this triangle to a pencil. Wrap the triangle around the pencil, and tape the end so that it doesn't unroll. Place your two homemade screws next to each other. Look at the thread lines formed by the new, longer slanted line. Does it look as though there are more lines on this pencil? How many more lines are there?

One of these homemade screws has more thread lines than the other.

Screws with Few Thread Lines

If a screw has few thread lines, its thread will cut into a material quickly and deeply. You don't have to turn the screw many times to tighten it. But it takes a lot of force to turn it.

. . . And with Many Thread Lines

If a screw has a lot of thread lines, its thread will not dig into the material as quickly or as deeply. You have to turn this screw more times to tighten it. But it is easier to turn. Why is it easier to turn a screw that has more thread lines? Let's find out.

A screw with few thread lines needs to be turned only a few times to tighten it. A screw with many thread lines needs to be turned many times to tighten it.

Put on Your Thinking Cap

Think about the two triangles you made. The triangle with the short, steep slant made only a few thread lines on your pencil. The triangle with the longer slant made more thread lines on your pencil.

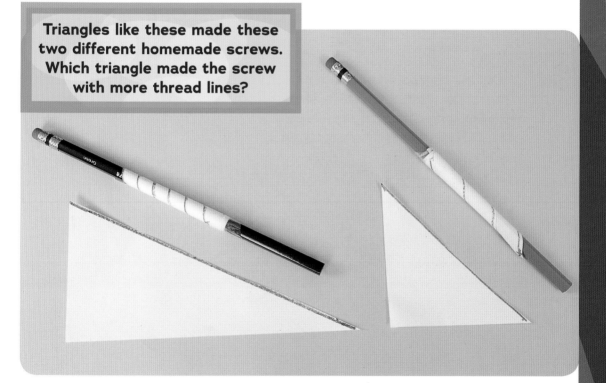

Triangles like these made these two different homemade screws. Which triangle made the screw with more thread lines?

Imagine that your triangles are two hills. It would be hard to climb the short, steep slope. Each step would take a lot of force. It would be easier to climb the longer slope. The longer slope is not as steep. You would walk a longer distance to reach the top. But each step would take only a little force.

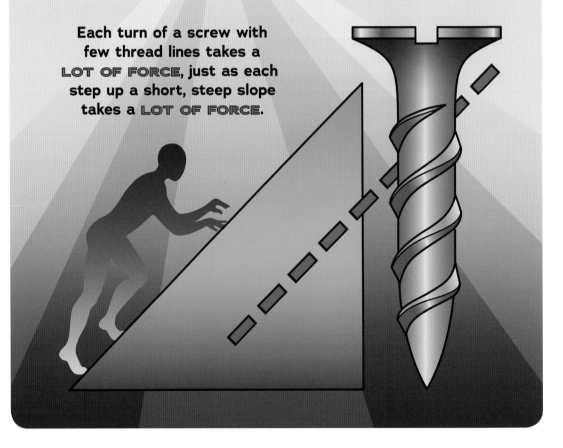

A SCREW'S THREAD IS LIKE A SLOPE

Each turn of a screw with few thread lines takes a LOT OF FORCE, just as each step up a short, steep slope takes a LOT OF FORCE.

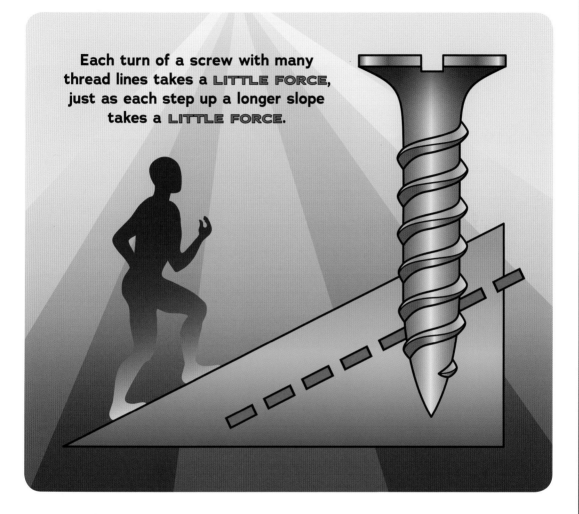

Each turn of a screw with many thread lines takes a LITTLE FORCE, just as each step up a longer slope takes a LITTLE FORCE.

Turning a screw with only a few thread lines is like climbing a steep hill. Each turn takes a lot of force. Turning a screw with many thread lines is like walking up a longer slope. The screw has to be turned more times. But each turn takes less force. That makes your work easier.

Screws: A Very Useful Tool

You have learned a lot about screws. Using this simple machine gives you an advantage. An advantage is a better chance of finishing your work.

Screws help us do many jobs.

Using a screw is almost like having a helper. And that's a real advantage.

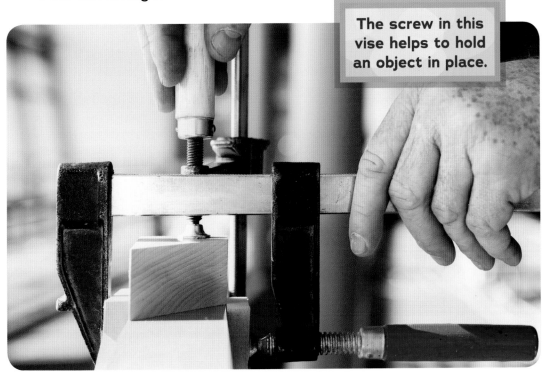

The screw in this vise helps to hold an object in place.

Glossary

complicated machine: a machine that has many moving parts. Clothes washers and electric drills are complicated machines.

force: a push or a pull. You use force to do chores, to play, and to eat.

screw: a simple machine that looks like a nail with ridges on it. The lids of some jars are also screws.

simple machine: a machine that has few moving parts. A screw is a simple machine.

thread: the ridges on a screw

work: using force to move an object from one place to another

Learn More about Simple Machines

Books

Challen, Paul C. *Get to Know Screws*. New York: Crabtree, 2009. This book discusses how screws work and how people use them.

Gosman, Gillian. *Screws in Action*. New York: PowerKids Press, 2011. Check out this title to see different examples of screws.

Manolis, Kay. *Screws*. Minneapolis: Bellwether Media, 2010. Find out more about screws in this selection.

Walker, Sally M., and Roseann Feldmann. *Put Wheels and Axles to the Test*. Minneapolis: Lerner Publications Company, 2012. Read all about wheels and axles, another important simple machine.

Way, Steve, and Gerry Bailey. *Simple Machines*. Pleasantville, NY: Gareth Stevens, 2009. This book explores a variety of simple machines, from wheels and axles to ramps and levers.

Websites

Quia—Simple Machines
http://www.quia.com/quiz/101964.html
Visit this site to find a challenging interactive quiz that allows budding physicists to test their knowledge of simple machines.

Simple Machines
http://sln.fi.edu/qa97/spotlight3/spotlight3.html
This website features brief information about simple machines and helpful links you can click on to learn more.

Index

Photo Acknowledgments

Photographs copyright © Andy King. Additional images are used with the permission of: © Fancy/Alamy, p. 5; © iStockphoto.com/Jill Fromer, p. 8; © Arne9001/Dreamstime.com, p. 9; © Mitar Holod/Dreamstime.com, p. 12; © Sean Macdiarmid/Dreamstime.com, p. 20; © Laura Westlund/Independent Picture Service, pp. 34, 35; © Andersen Ross/Digital Vision/Getty Images, p. 37.

Front cover: © Inger Anne Hulbækdal/Dreamstime.com.

Main body text set in Adrianna Regular 14/20.
Typeface provided by Chank.